Frank is a tough man. He laughs. He hits Len on the head. He hits Len hard. Len's eyes close. Len falls down. He falls onto the floor of the office.

Mr Blane gives Len a photo. He says,
'I want Carmen back. Go to the bus station
at two o'clock on Tuesday. Frank has
the $100 000. He's going with you.
Give the money to The Young Ones.
Bring Carmen home. I'll pay you $1000.'

Len says, 'I don't like you, Blane.
I don't want your money. But
Carmen is in trouble. She needs help.
I'll help her.'

It's 2 pm on Tuesday. Frank and Len are at the bus station. Frank has $100 000 in a bag.

Large buses are going in and out of the bus station. There are lots of people. But Len can't see Carmen.

Frank opens the bag. The young man sees the money. The young man lets go of Carmen's arm.

Len holds Carmen's arm. Frank gives the bag of money to the young man.

Suddenly, Carmen bites Len's hand.
Len lets go of Carmen's arm.

The young man hits Frank.
Frank falls down.

Carmen and the young man jump onto the bus. The door of the bus closes. The bus drives off. It's going to San Francisco.

SAN FRANCISCO

Len can't get on the bus. He decides to get his car. Len decides to drive to San Francisco.

12

It's Thursday. Len is in San Francisco. San Francisco is a big city. Len can't find Carmen.

Suddenly, Len sees a sign on a building.

The sign says: The Young Ones. The building is a school for poor children. Carmen is playing with the children.

Len stops his car. He goes to speak to Carmen.

14